Be a Zillionaire

The Young Zillionaire's Guide to

Supply and Demand

David Seidman

the rosen publishing group's
rosen
central

To a man who helps me with my customers:
my attorney, Paul Levine.

Published in 2000 by The Rosen Publishing Group, Inc.
29 East 21st Street, New York, NY 10010

First Edition

Library of Congress Cataloging-in-Publication Data

Seidman, David
    The young zillionaire's guide to supply and demand / David Seidman.
      p.   cm. — (Be a zillionaire)
    Includes bibliographical references and index.
    Summary: Provides information on the basics of supply and demand and the role of supply and demand in the economy.
    ISBN 0-8239-3264-8
    1. Supply and Demand—Juvenile literature. [1. Supply and demand.] I. Title. II. Series.

Manufactured in the United States of America

TABLE OF CONTENTS

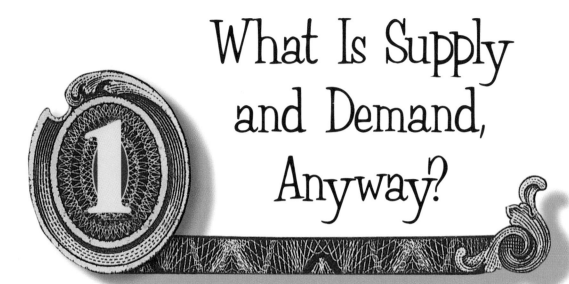

What Is Supply and Demand, Anyway?

This is a book for anyone who has ever wondered how people get rich. Just about everyone who becomes rich uses knowledge about supply and demand, and you can, too.

But what is supply and demand?

Supply

Supply is any product that a seller offers for sale. When most people think of products, they think of objects: abacuses, accordions, apples, aspirin tablets, avocados—and that's just the As.

Experience

But objects aren't the only products: There's also experience. When you buy a ticket to get on a roller coaster, you expect to get a few minutes of thrills. When you go to a movie, take a vacation, or rent shoes at a bowling alley, you're buying an experience.

Service

Another kind of product is service. What's the difference between buying

When you go to a movie, you're buying an experience.

chicken wings at a grocery store and buying them at Kentucky Fried Chicken? The KFC workers have supplied a service: They've cooked the wings. And so it goes with everyone who works for a living. Each of them supplies a service to his or her employer.

Much of this book will treat you as if you're running your own business—that is, as if you're a seller. But even if you work for someone else, you're selling him or her a product—or, rather, your services, whether the service is flipping burgers or giving investment advice.

Financial Products

Then there are the things that bankers call "financial products"—for instance, money. If you want a dollar (and who doesn't?), would you pay more than a dollar to get it? Surprisingly, for many people the answer is yes.

Let's say that you have no money with you, but you want to buy something that costs a dollar. You could borrow that dollar from your pal Len, but he might say, "Sure, I'll supply you the dollar—but I charge a quarter to do it. When you pay me back, you have to pay me a dollar and a quarter."

Len may not be your most warm-hearted friend, but his offer resembles the way that banks and credit card companies work: They, too, charge a price to lend money.

And so it goes with other products. A supplier, also called a producer or seller, tries to sell products to a demander—otherwise known as a consumer, customer, or buyer.

And speaking of demanders . . .

Demand

Demand is the buyer's willingness to pay for a product. To put it simply, demand is desire plus money.

The money part is crucial. Harry wants a mansion; Rita the real estate agent sells mansions. But Harry has no money, and Rita's in business to make money. So Harry's desire doesn't matter to Rita. As far as she's concerned, Harry's desire may as well not exist at all. He has no true demand.

Harry's desire becomes a true demand only if he

backs it up with enough money to buy a mansion. If Rita—or any seller—finds buyers with a genuine, cash-fueled demand to buy her product, she can get rich.

Price

Price is where demand meets supply. If a seller offers to sell a product at a price that a buyer is willing to pay, then the buyer gets the product, the seller gets the buyer's money, and everyone is happy.

Price is also the way that sellers find out how much demand a product generates. When Gretchen the grocer offers onions at 10¢ apiece, her customers buy lots of onions. Gretchen figures that there's a lot of demand

Price is where demand meets supply.

for onions, so she raises the price to $1 apiece—and the customers stop buying. If Gretchen is smart, she'll soon realize, "There's lots of demand for onions at a low price, but not much demand for them at a high price."

Then Gretchen may wonder: "If people will buy an onion for a dime, how about a quarter? Or 50 cents? How high can I raise the price before people stop buying the product?" Gretchen is seeking the price that every seller wants: the market clearing price.

The Slippery Market Clearing Price (MCP)

The market clearing price, or MCP, is the highest price that a seller can charge and still sell all of his or her products. It literally clears the seller out of his or her supply. It clears out the demand, too, because the MCP is low enough for the buyers to buy as much of the product as they want. Under the MCP, the supply perfectly satisfies the demand.

You might think that once the seller finds the MCP, he or she will get rich. But the MCP moves. For example,

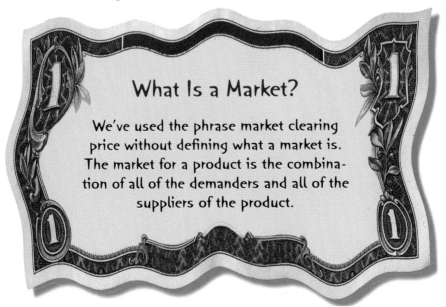

What Is a Market?

We've used the phrase market clearing price without defining what a market is. The market for a product is the combination of all of the demanders and all of the suppliers of the product.

imagine that you run a shoe store. You offer shoes at $100 per pair, and your customers buy most of them. You say to yourself, "If I lower the shoes' price, people can afford to buy more shoes, and I'll sell more of them." You lower the shoes' price to $99.99, and your customers buy all of them. "Aha!" you say. "$99.99 is the market clearing price!" So you order more shoes, you price them at $99.99, and no one buys them. What's happening?

Your customers have gone across the street to a store that has started selling the same shoes at $90 per pair. If you want to sell your shoes, you'd better sell them for no more than $90—the new MCP.

Business is full of this sort of slippery terrain. The next few chapters will help you get a firm footing on it.

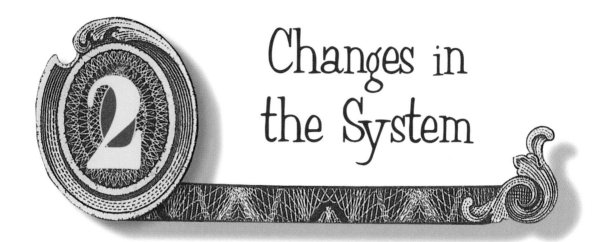

Changes in the System

Markets never hold still. Prices rise and fall, demand climbs and slides, and supply grows and shrinks. What's a simple, honest businessperson to do?

He or she can start by understanding how it all works. But hang on: It can be a bumpy ride.

A Rise in Demand

Every few years, there's a new trend in music. Imagine that next year, young bands start playing a fresh hybrid of blues and rap that they call blap. Rudolph, manager of Rudolph's Records, notices that his customers are buying a lot of blap records.

Clearly, the demand for blap is rising.

Rudolph wants to take advantage of the demand, so he raises the prices on his blap records. When the demand for a product rises, the seller raises the product's price.

To make as much money as he can, Rudolph orders a lot more blap records. When the demand for a product

When demand for a product rises, the seller raises the products price.

rises, the seller increases the supply of the product. But Rudolph isn't the only one who notices the popularity of blap. Other music stores increase their supply of blap records. When the demand for a product rises, competing sellers increase their supply of the product.

What's more, sellers that don't usually carry blap—bookstores, cafes, even Gretchen the grocer—start offering blap records to their customers. When the demand for a product rises, new competitors enter the market and start to offer the product.

This rise in the amount of the product demonstrates

the law of supply: Suppliers offer more of a product at a high price than at a low one.

A Rise in Supply

The demand for blap not only drives up the supply, it also drives up the price from $15 a record to $20. But people who were willing to buy a record at $15 don't want to pay $20. This arrangement is the law of demand: As price rises, demand falls.

Meanwhile, Rudolph and other sellers are offering more and more blap records, thousands of them. Rudolph notices that people aren't buying as many as he had hoped. Clearly, the supply is higher than the demand. Though blap is popular enough to sell hundreds of records, it's not popular enough to sell thousands. When it's time for Rudolph to order new records, he reduces his orders for blap. So do the other sellers. When the supply of a product rises faster than the demand for it, the seller lowers the supply.

But what about the blap records that are already clogging Rudolph's store? To get them off his hands, Rudolph lowers their price from $20 to $5. So do the other sellers. When the supply of a product rises faster than the demand for it, the seller lowers the price.

People who wouldn't buy a blap record at $20 or $15 are happy to buy it at $5. The lower price has raised the demand.

That's the flip side to the law of demand: As price falls, demand rises. Then the whole cycle starts over again.

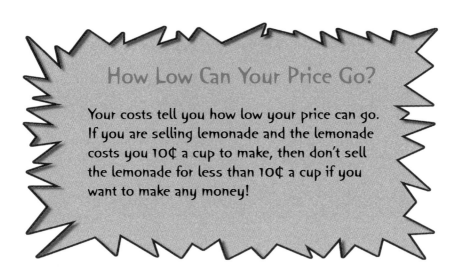

How Low Can Your Price Go?

Your costs tell you how low your price can go. If you are selling lemonade and the lemonade costs you 10¢ a cup to make, then don't sell the lemonade for less than 10¢ a cup if you want to make any money!

The Endless Circle

 A rise in demand causes the price and the supply to rise.

 The rise in supply causes the price to fall.

 The fall in price causes demand to rise.

 And so on and so on and so on.

To make money within this cycle, get in early and get out early. That is, increase your supply as demand starts to rise, and cut your price as demand starts to fall. If you increase your supply to meet the rising demand, you can satisfy the demand and make good money. If you don't increase your supply, then your customers will ask you, "Do you have the product that I want?"—and you'll have to say, "No, I don't." The customers will give their money to someone who does have a supply of the product.

Where Can You Get Your Supply?

If you notice a big demand for a product, you'll want to get your hands on a big supply of the product. You can find the producers of almost any product in the yellow pages, on the Internet, or in business magazines.

You may even be able to produce the product yourself. If your neighbor has a high demand for people to rake leaves, then you can supply that product by offering to do the raking yourself.

If you cut your price as demand falls, you'll be able to grab all of what little demand is left. If you don't cut your price, then your customers will say (to themselves, if not to you), "I want this product, but I don't want it enough to pay a high price." The customers will walk away without giving you any money.

But how can you tell when demand will start to rise or fall? And even more important, how can you make it rise?

Curious? Check out the next chapter for some answers.

What Makes Demand Rise and Fall?

If you listen to economists on TV news shows (great for those nights when you can't get to sleep), you might conclude that supply and demand has everything to do with prices and products but nothing to do with people. That conclusion is false, mostly. A lot of raw, juicy human behavior drives supply and demand.

Customer Preference

Customer preference—or taste—is possibly the most basic source of demand. If you want vanilla ice cream and you're ready to pay for it, someone will sell it to you. The smart seller looks for changes in customer taste and gets a supply of products that fit those tastes.

You can find out your customers' tastes by noticing which of your products—and your competitors' products—sell best. You can also ask your customers what they want.

General Motors did just that a few years ago and found that car buyers wanted a friendly, low-pressure atmosphere at car dealerships. So GM created Saturn, which it called "a different kind of car company." Saturn dealers sell cars with friendliness and low pressure, and as a result, Saturn became a success.

Changing Tastes

But be careful. Customer tastes can be fickle. If you sell ice cream, you may notice that your customers demand vanilla ice cream. You stock up on a huge supply of vanilla. Then you find that your customers are suddenly bored with vanilla and eager for banana nut. Changes in customer taste can cause demand to rise or fall unexpectedly.

If you find that customer taste has moved away from your products, you can still raise the demand for them. How? One of the most basic ways is price.

Changes in customer taste can cause demand to rise and fall.

Price

If you've ever gone to garage sales, you've seen the power of price. People will buy stuff at a garage sale that they'd never buy in a store, simply because the price is too low to pass up. The low price has increased the demand. To raise the demand for a product, lower its price.

But wait—you may not want to lower the price right away. Let's say that you sell vanilla ice cream at $1 per scoop. Demand is high; you sell one hundred scoops a day. Then customer taste shifts away from vanilla, making the demand fall until you sell only ten scoops a day. So you cut the price to 50¢ per scoop.

At a price that low, demand rises for vanilla until you're selling one hundred scoops a day again. You're eager to take advantage of the high demand, so you raise the price back to $1—but now you're selling no scoops at all. "Wait a minute," you complain. "The last time that the price was $1 a scoop, I sold ten scoops a day. Now the price is $1 again, so why aren't I selling ten scoops again? Why am I selling nothing?"

Your customers have caught on to you. They know that you can sell vanilla at 50¢ a scoop, so they're no longer willing to pay a buck for a scoop. To sell vanilla, you have to go back down to 50¢.

If you lower your prices, you can raise demand, but lowering prices can trap you into keeping the prices low whether you want to or not. So cut prices carefully.

Don't do it too soon, too often, or too deeply. After all, there are other ways to raise demand.

Quality

This one is simple: Most people have more demand for a good product than for a poor one. Japanese car makers broke into the tight U.S. market by making cars that were safer and longer-lasting than American cars. Demand for these superior machines pulled demand away from American cars.

If you can make a better version of an existing product, or create a new product that works better than an existing product, then you can make customers demand your product. Another way to increase demand is to add features to an existing product. If customers have a demand for a VCR that plays tapes, they may have a greater demand for a VCR that plays tapes and records TV shows, and an even greater demand for a VCR that plays tapes, records TV shows, and has concert-quality sound.

Ease and Difficulty

If your product is difficult to buy, you can increase the demand for it by making it easy to buy. Most people won't travel 100 miles to buy apples. But they will go 10 feet. If your customers can find you and your product easily and quickly, you're not just selling a product. You're also selling ease and convenience. Those qualities are always in demand.

In that sense, difficulty of purchase is a kind of price. If you want to buy another copy of this book, you go to your local bookstore. If the book isn't there, you search from store to store. After an hour of searching, you find the book. The book's cover price is $15—but the real price that you pay is $15 plus your hour of searching.

People know that their time is valuable. If you ordinarily earn $10 per hour, the price of the book isn't exactly $15; it's $15 plus $10, or $25. You might pay $16 to buy the book right away rather than $15 for a copy that will take you an hour to find.

The time you spend searching for a product is part of its price.

Short Supply

As you can already see, demand is slippery. It can easily move out of a seller's hands, especially when the seller doesn't have enough product to satisfy the demand.

Let's say that Walter goes to his local hardware store to buy left-handed monkey wrenches. The store doesn't have enough wrenches—that is, the wrenches are in short supply at that store. He takes his demand to another store, which has a bigger supply.

To make money from such a situation, a smart businessperson would find out which products are in high demand and short supply, and then stock up on them. To find out which items are in high demand and short supply, listen to customer complaints. When you hear a customer complain that he or she can't find a product, that's your cue to get the product and sell it to him or her.

Or, rather, it's usually your cue. But not always. Imagine that Cynthia goes into a store to buy a candy bar made of caramel, cream, and cashews: the CarCrash. Morris, the man behind the counter, tells Cynthia that he's sold out of CarCrashes. Cynthia leaves.

You're in the store, too. You think, "If I can get a CarCrash to satisfy Cynthia's demand, I'll make a little money." You run to another store that sells CarCrashes, buy one, and take it to Cynthia. You offer her the bar, but she says, "No, thanks. I had a quick urge for the bar, but the urge is gone now." Cynthia's demand has faded, and you're stuck with a CarCrash.

This example demonstrates another key point about supply and demand: Demand connected to short supply can slip away fast, so satisfy the demand while it is happening. If you don't have the product at the moment when a customer demands it, then you can lose the customer.

Some sellers even keep extra supplies of products that don't sell very well, in case the demand for the products suddenly shoots up. These sellers are trying not to get caught with short supply.

Substitutes

Let's go back to the moment when Morris told Cynthia, "Sorry, we're out of CarCrashes." Instead of letting Cynthia leave his store without buying anything, what if Morris had said, "Try this new bar instead. It tastes like a CarCrash. It's called a Fishing Trip. One bite and you'll be hooked!"?

Cynthia buys the Fishing Trip, likes it, and buys six more. She forgets about the CarCrash. Then Morris promotes the Fishing Trip to all of his customers. Demand for Fishing Trips rises, whereas demand for CarCrashes falls. From this you can see yet another principle of buying and selling: A substitute product can pull demand away from the original product.

Producers know this fact well. They also know that when demand for a supplier's product rises, competing suppliers make substitutes for that product. For example, when personal computers first became popular and the demand for them rose, the makers of other office machines noticed. To siphon off some of the demand, they created similar machines.

Why do consumers buy substitute products? Sometimes there isn't enough supply of the original products. Usually, though, there is enough supply of the originals, but the substitutes are sold at a lower price. The lower price will raise the demand for the substitutes.

Complements and Derived Demand

When the demand for hot dogs rises, the demand for hot dog buns rises. When the demand for cars rises, the demand for gasoline rises. When the demand for wedding rings rises, the demand for wedding gowns rises. These items are all complements.

Complements are products that fit together so well that when the demand for one of the products rises, the demand for the other product usually rises, too. They're called complements because when put together, they form a complete package.

When the demand for hot dogs rises, the demand for buns rises.

Derived Demand

Some products that look like complements aren't, exactly. If the demand for books rises, then the demand for paper to print the books will rise. But if the demand for paper rises, the demand for books may not rise because people who demand paper may plan to use it as stationery or other things that aren't books. This one-way-street kind of demand is called derived demand.

The sharp businessperson looks at the demand for a product to figure out if it generates complementary demand or derived demand for other products. If the students at your school start wearing clothes that light up, there will be a derived demand for electricity, so you could sell them batteries. If they switch to edible fabrics made of hot peppers and chilies, sell cold drinks. If they change to clothes made of razor blades, sell bandages.

Marginal Demand

When you buy a product, you expect to get a benefit from it. For instance, you buy a dinner to fill your belly. Once the dinner fills you up, you don't usually turn immediately around and buy another dinner. Once a customer buys a product, his or her demand for another unit of that product usually falls.

But the demand doesn't always fall very far. That's where margin comes in. Margin is the difference between the demand for the first unit of a product and the demand for the next unit. And margin can mean money.

Rita the real estate agent sells a house to Carl the client. As Carl moves in, the local power company sells him electricity. The house gives Carl all of the housing that he needs, so he won't buy another house for many years. But his house needs electricity every minute, so he'll buy one kilowatt after another. The marginal demand for another house is very low; the marginal demand for another kilowatt is very high.

A smart seller knows how much marginal demand her product has. With that knowledge, she figures out when to offer another unit of the product. Rita will wait years to offer Carl a new house; the power company will offer him power all the time.

Advertising

For customers to demand a product, they have to know about it. Advertising tells them about it.

North Carolina's Food Lion chain of grocery stores was having a hard time competing against other grocers. So the chain started offering lower prices than other stores and putting the slogan LFPINC (Lowest Food Prices in North Carolina) in its advertisements. As a result, Food Lion's sales grew to more than $6 billion a year.

A seller has to show potential buyers the benefits that his or her product has over other products. Food Lion stressed the benefit of low price. Other producers might advertise convenience, service, or quality.

Income

Low prices create high demand. But a price that seems low to a rich person can seem high to a poor one.

24

Tina earns $20,000 per year. She wants to buy a car. She goes to a car dealership and sees a car that she likes, but it costs $20,000. She has no demand for a car with so high a price, so she walks away. Suddenly, Tina gets a new job. Now she makes $200,000 per year. She buys the car. Her demand for the car rose, even though the car and its price never changed.

Why? Because price is a portion of the consumer's income. For Tina, the car's price fell, even though it stayed at $20,000. It fell from being worth all of her income to being worth only a tenth of it.

For Tina—as well as for everyone else—rising income leads to rising demand. A seller who wants to make money should set up shop where people have rising incomes.

On the other hand, falling income leads to falling demand. So stay away from places where people are losing their jobs. They won't have money to give you.

Finally . . .

If you follow the insights in this chapter, you should have as much demand for your products as you can handle. But watch out. Every other businessperson is out to increase demand for his or her own products. This desire can create some odd circumstances, which the next chapter explains.

Exceptions and Other Weird Twists

The laws of supply and demand apply to all aspects of business. But you may see some suppliers and demanders who don't obey the laws. At least that's how it seems.

Paradoxes of Price

Raising a product's price usually lowers the demand for the product. But sometimes raising prices can raise the demand. Take luxury items, for example. One benefit that buyers get from buying a high-priced product is the chance to brag about how high its price is. ("Our new house cost a million dollars, and then my parents spent another million on the pool and tennis courts. Pretty cool, huh?" or "Look at this engagement ring my fiancé gave me! It set him back ten thousand bucks!")

Economists have complex explanations for these situations. A businessperson, though, can handle them simply by understanding his or her customers. Some customers want to show the world how rich they are ("Our new house cost a million dollars . . ."), and that desire matters more to them than the desire to get a low price.

Sometimes, as with luxury items, raising prices can raise the demand.

Others like to show off their generosity, like the fiancé who gave his girlfriend an expensive ring. If you know your customers, you can find out what desires make them spend money and use those desires to make them spend it on your products.

Meanwhile, a low price usually raises demand—but not always. Low-price items are often poorly made. So when customers see an item at an especially low price, they may expect shoddy quality: "You're selling VCRs for only fifty bucks? There must be something wrong with them. I don't want to buy one."

If you sell items at a low price, and you sense that your customers distrust your price, you can soften their suspicions through advertising. Tell them your reasons for keeping the price low: Customer tastes have changed, or a cheap substitute for your product has come onto the market and you have to match its low price.

And speaking of low price . . .

Stockpiling: A Paradox of Demand

You might expect people to spend a low amount of money on a product at a low price. Actually, they often spend a high amount at a low price.

For example: You run a drugstore. You usually price a tube of toothpaste at $2. Most of your customers buy a $2 tube every month. But for some reason, one month you get an extra large supply of toothpaste. To lower the supply, you decrease the price to $1.

Your customers know that a price that low doesn't come around every day. They also suspect that the sale won't last long. So instead of buying the usual single tube, each customer buys three tubes, spending $3 when they'd ordinarily spend $2. This is called stockpiling: Although the price is lower than usual, the customers have actually spent more money than usual.

A customer will stockpile products only if the products can sit on the customer's shelf for a long time without losing any value. Perishable items, on the other hand, can't be stockpiled. Bananas, for instance, turn brown and become inedible after a few days. A small family won't buy one hundred bananas no matter how low the price goes.

Elasticity

Remember this?

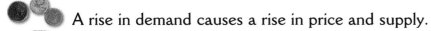 A rise in demand causes a rise in price and supply.

 The rise in supply causes the price to fall.

 The fall in price causes demand to rise.

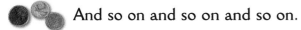 And so on and so on and so on.

Although their rise and fall are connected, supply, price, and demand don't always rise and fall in the same amounts. Sometimes demand rises a lot, but supply rises only a little. Sometimes prices fall a huge amount, but demand rises only a tiny amount. The difference between these factors is called elasticity. Elasticity can help to determine how much money a seller can make.

For instance, let's say that dog breeders develop a new breed of dog, a cross between a Newfoundland and a Yorkshire terrier, known as a New York. At first, New Yorks are very expensive. Only movie stars and other rich and fashionable people buy them.

To raise the demand, dog breeders drop the price of New Yorks a little. At the same time, everyone in the country sees movie stars walking their New Yorks, and everybody wants their own New York. Though the price has fallen only a little, the demand for New Yorks rises a lot. The demand is more elastic than the price.

The breeders, noticing the rise in demand, raise their prices a little. They expect the demand to fall a little. But they find that their customers are buying poodles instead of New Yorks. The New Yorks' popularity was only a passing fad, and it passed. Though the price has risen a little, the demand falls a lot. Once again, the demand is more elastic than the price.

Elasticity and Substitutes

Elasticity is based on substitutes. The more substitutes for a product—poodles, goldfish, whatever—the more elastic the demand for the product. If you're selling a product, and you see plenty of substitutes for the product, expect the demand for the product to fall.

Demand isn't always elastic. In 1986, Japanese paper manufacturer Ryoei Saito paid $82.5 million for Vincent Van Gogh's *Portrait du Dr. Gachet*—the highest price ever paid for a painting. Even though high prices usually make demand shrink, the price of the portrait clearly didn't make Saito's demand shrink. As the price rose, his demand remained the same. That is, his demand was inelastic.

What makes the demand for a product inelastic? A lack of substitutes. Van Gogh painted very few works that still exist, and he can't paint any more because he's dead. There aren't many substitutes for the work of a person like that.

Van Gogh's art is an example of inelastic supply. The supply of Van Gogh's paintings can't grow, no matter how high the demand rises.

The supply of Van Gogh's paintings is inelastic. It can't grow, no matter how high the demand rises.

Supply, Demand, and Elasticity

Demand is usually more elastic than supply. As we've seen, demand can change very easily and quickly; all it takes is a public whim. But creating a supply of a product can be costly and time-consuming—or sometimes, as in the case of Van Gogh's paintings, impossible.

Monopolies, Oligopolies, and Cartels

Monopoly means one seller. If you're the only person selling a product, you're running a monopoly.

Thomas Edison had a monopoly on moviemaking for years.

Monopolies

If you run a monopoly, you can raise prices whenever you want and keep the quality of your product low because your customers have no other place to get your product. They'll buy it no matter what. A lot of businesspeople would love to run monopolies.

Businesspeople create monopolies by inventing products that no one else has. For instance, Thomas Edison had a monopoly on moviemaking for years. He was one of the chief inventors of the movie camera and the process of shooting a film; anyone who wanted to make movies had to pay him a fee. Edison was based in New Jersey, and the movie business was based in nearby New York City, where Edison could keep an eye on moviemakers and force them to pay up. His monopoly stayed in place until moviemakers fled to California, where Edison couldn't catch them.

Another way to create a monopoly is to buy out anyone who's making a similar or substitute product. Industrialist J.P. Morgan bought out (or otherwise came to control) so many steel companies that his mammoth United States Steel company more or less owned America's steel industry. It took the federal government to stop him.

Some variations on the monopoly are the oligopoly and cartel.

Oligopolies

In an oligopoly, there are only a few suppliers of a product. In the early 1950s, the American auto industry was an oligopoly in that three automakers—Ford, General Motors, and Chrysler—ruled the market. Smaller American companies were dying, and foreign companies hadn't yet dug deep into the U.S. market.

Cartels

In a cartel, there may be lots of suppliers of a product—but instead of competing as suppliers usually do, they work together. They limit the supply of the product in order to drive up the demand. De Beers, a South African mining company, runs the best-known modern cartel: It dominates the companies that mine diamonds, restricts the supply, and pushes up the price, making a diamond engagement ring one of the highest costs of getting married.

Fighting Back

If you find that your competitors are building a monopoly, oligopoly, or cartel, how can you stop them?

Use all of the methods that generate demand:

If only one person in your town sells ice cream, be more attuned to customer tastes than she is; offer flavors that her customers like better.

Make a higher-quality product; maybe your ice cream is sweeter than hers.

Add complementary products; if your competitor sells ice cream with only one topping, then offer lots of different toppings.

Offer the customers a lower price; if your competitor charges a buck a scoop, charge 90¢.

Offer a substitute product; sell frozen yogurt rather than or in addition to ice cream.

Offer convenience; place your ice-cream stand at a location that's closer to the customers than your competitor's locations.

Substitutes or No Substitutes?

There are substitutes for virtually everything—if the customer is willing to accept them. As far as Ryoei Saito was concerned, there were virtually no substitutes for Van Gogh's <u>Portrait du Dr. Gachet.</u> That's a reason that he paid so much for it.

But other buyers might accept a substitute—another Van Gogh painting, or one of his pencil sketches, or the work of another painter. A smart seller always tries to find out which substitute products his or her customers are willing to buy.

You can also go to the law. Since monopolies are illegal in the United States, you can sue a monopolist or file a complaint with the government.

All of which brings us to the next chapter.

Supply and Demand on a Large Scale

As billions of people raise and lower the demand, price, and supply of billions of products, they generate some monster-size effects. Anyone who wants to get rich should be ready for these economic earthquakes.

Recession

A recession is a period when demand is much lower than supply. In a recession, businesses can't sell much and lose lots of money. Of course, businesses can go broke at any time. The difference between an ordinary business slowdown and a recession is that the recession lasts for months and strikes many markets at the same time.

Recessions often happen after wars, since wars affect a vast sweep of businesses. During a war, the government has a huge demand for rifles, uniforms, and thousands of other products. It also has a demand for soldiers, sailors, and other workers. When the war ends, however, the demand for all of these products stops cold. The government suddenly discharges millions of troops, filling the country with jobless veterans. Supply is high, demand is low, and the veterans don't have enough money to drive demand up again. That's a recipe for recession.

Beating Recession

What can a businessperson do when a recession hits? Since a recession is a time of low demand, use every method to raise demand, especially cutting prices.

Also, remember that no matter how widely a recession spreads, some people will still have money. If you can discover and satisfy the demands of the wealthy, you can escape the worst of a recession.

Finally, smart businesspeople know that recessions come every few years—there were recessions in 1970, 1974–75, 1982, and 1990–91—so they save their money during the prosperous times between recessions. As a result, when recessions hit, they don't go broke. They have enough money to withstand the fall in demand and income that a recession brings.

Inflation

You've probably heard the word "inflation" before, but do you know what it means? Inflation is the condition that arises when sellers in all parts of the economy raise their prices. The prices are, so to speak, inflating: They're expanding and rising like a hot-air balloon.

Inflation can be as disastrous as recession. If you earn $50,000 per year, and all of your expenses—food, clothing, shelter, and so on—cost you $40,000 a year, then you're making a nice, fat $10,000 profit. But if the price of your expenses rises to $60,000, and your earnings remain at $50,000, then you're losing $10,000.

Supply Shock

A main cause of inflation is supply shock. Supply shock is a big, fast, sudden fall in the supply of a product without a similar fall in demand. In 1973, for example, a cartel of oil producers cut off the supply of oil to the United States. Though the supply of oil was suddenly low, the demand was high, which made oil prices rise high and fast. Since oil is a part of more than one section of the economy, from automobiles to home heating, the rise in oil prices triggered a rise in prices elsewhere. The result? Inflation.

Supply shock, by the way, is also called cost-push inflation, since the cost of products (oil, for instance) pushes prices up.

Demand-Pull Inflation

A similar phenomenon to supply shock is demand-pull, in which the supply of a product doesn't rise much, but the demand rises a lot. If the government prints a lot of money, for instance, buyers will have a lot of money to spend, and their demand for products will rise. As demand rises, it pulls price up with it. If prices go up in all parts of the economy, you get inflation.

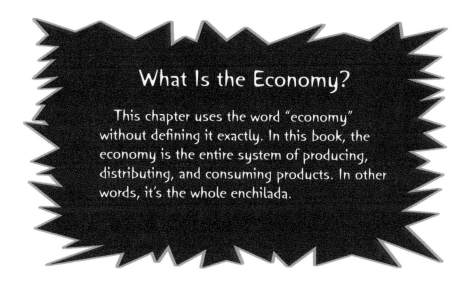

What Is the Economy?

This chapter uses the word "economy" without defining it exactly. In this book, the economy is the entire system of producing, distributing, and consuming products. In other words, it's the whole enchilada.

Handling Inflation

If you're a businessperson, how can you handle inflation? You can raise your prices as fast as the rate of inflation rises. That's dangerous, of course, since your customers may not have enough money to pay your rising prices.

You can also invest in items whose value rises faster than the rate of inflation. Let's say that inflation rises by 10 percent per year, so that a concert ticket that costs $10 at the beginning of January will cost $11 at the end of December. The United States government may offer a savings bond that pays 15 percent interest—in other words, if you buy a $10 bond in January, you can cash it in for $15 in December. Since $15 is more than $11, the savings bond beats the rate of inflation, and it's a good investment.

The Role of the Government

Government always affects business. Every law that it passes or declines to pass, every patent that it grants or refuses, and every regulation that it enforces or fails to enforce will change the supply, demand, or price of at least one product.

For instance, the government can outlaw a product. If the government outlaws a drug, then buying the drug or selling it can land you in jail. Imprisonment is too high a price for most people to pay. It can cause their demand for the drug to fall.

On the other hand, the government can make a product mandatory. Some years ago, the government decreed that new cars must include air bags in the front seat to cushion the impact of crashes. Suddenly, automakers had to buy air bags, which raised the demand for the product.

Government regulation raised demand for air bags.

In addition to passing laws, the government can enter the market. We've already seen what happens in wartime: The government raises its demand for soldiers, equipment, and other products, and drops the demand for them when peace comes.

Indirect Effects

But the government can have other, less direct effects, too. If it launches antidrug advertisements, it may lower the demand for drugs. If it makes confusing laws, it can raise the demand for lawyers who help citizens understand the laws. If it cracks down on crime in a dangerous neighborhood, it can turn the area into a safe place where everyone wants to live, and drive up the demand for land and buildings in the area.

Finally, the government can change the supply of the most demanded product of all: money. Only the government is allowed to supply money; competitors are called counterfeiters and the government tries to shut them down. The government has a monopoly over money.

The government can print extra dollars, increasing the money supply. This action can trigger inflation. The government also can raise taxes, pulling money out of the economy and decreasing the supply of dollars in the citizens' hands. Since reducing the amount of a person's money can reduce his or her demand for products, a sharp drop in the amount of money in the whole economy can spark a recession.

A Word to the Wise

What does the government's power mean to the would-be zillionaire? Two words: Pay attention. Read the newspapers. Keep an eye on what the government is doing. If you acquire a supply of a product and you discover that the government has outlawed it, then get rid of the product immediately. Don't sell it, even if the demand is high. It's better to lose your supply than to go to jail.

Invest wisely!

If the government raises the demand for a product, then get a supply of that product—providing that the product is legal, of course. If the government seems likely to flood the economy with dollars and cause inflation, then invest wisely, and raise your prices to keep up with the inflation rate.

If the government seems likely to send your taxes higher, you'll need a higher supply of money to pay the taxes. To raise the money, you may need to raise the demand for your product.

And if it seems that the government may set off a recession, prepare as you would for any recession. Stockpile cash, find out where the demand for your products will be, and ride out the recession as best you can.

Okay, so now you know that it's not that easy to get rich. Let's face it: If it were easy, almost everybody would do it.

But you've done something that not everybody does. You've put in the time and effort to read this book. You know more than most people about supply and demand.

There's much more to learn, of course. Much of it you'll find out as you dive in and start to supply a product, set a price for it, and find a demand for it. Good luck!

GLOSSARY

demand The buyer's willingness to pay for a product; demand is desire plus money.

demand-pull When the demand for a product rises faster than the supply.

economy The entire system of producing, distributing, and consuming products.

elasticity The difference between the rise and fall of supply, price, and demand.

inflation The condition when sellers in all parts of the economy raise their prices.

law of demand As price falls, demand rises.

law of supply Suppliers offer more of a product at a high price than at a low one.

margin The difference between the demand for the first unit of a product and the demand for the next unit.

opportunity cost What customers must give up in order to have what they want.

price The point at which demand meets supply.

recession A long period when demand is much lower than supply.

supply Any product that a seller offers for sale.

FOR MORE INFORMATION

Web Sites

A. G. Edwards' Big Money Adventure
http://www.agedwards.com/bma/index.shtml

I Can Buy
http://www.icanbuy.com

Kidsense
http://www.kidsenseonline.com
http://www.nuveen.com

Save Lab
http://www.plan.ml.com/family/kids

Young Investors Network
http://www.salomonsmithbarney.com/yin

The Young Investor Web Site
http://www.younginvestor.com/pick.shtml

For Further Reading

Bangs, David H. Jr., and Linda Pinson. *The Real World Entrepreneur Field Guide*. New York: Upstart Press, 1999.

The Economist Guide to Economic Indicators. New York: Wiley & Sons, 1997.

Giesbrecht, Martin Gerhard, and Gary E. Clayton. *A Guide to Everyday Economic Thinking*. New York: McGraw-Hill, 1997.

Godfrey, Neale S. *Neale S. Godfrey's Ultimate Kids' Money Book*. New York: Simon & Schuster, 1998.

Kidron, Michael, and Ronald Segal. *What You Need to Know About Business, Money and Power*. New York: Simon & Schuster, 1987.

Lee, Susan. *Susan Lee's ABZs of Economics*. New York: Pocket Books, 1987.

Mariotti, Steve, with Tony Towle and Debra DeSalvo. *The Young Entrepreneur's Guide to Starting and Running a Small Business*. New York: Times/Random House, 1996.

INDEX

Acknowledgments

I'd like to thank the following libraries, which gave me the information that I needed to write this book: Beverly Hills Public Library; Los Angeles Public Library, Robertson and West Los Angeles branches; UCLA University Research Library; UCLA College Library; Los Angeles County Library, West Hollywood branch.

Thanks to one and all.

Photo Credits

Cover photos © Artville; pp. 5, 11 by Shalhevet Moshe; pp. 7, 19 by Thaddeus Harden; p. 16 © Richard T. Nowitz/Corbis; p. 22 © 1999 Nova Development Corporation; p. 27 © Gail Mooney/Corbis; pp. 31, 32, 42 © FPG International Stock; p. 40 © Richard Olivier/Corbis.

Series Design

Law Alsobrook

Layout Design

Danielle Goldblatt